Knowings from The Silence Vol. 3

Even More Simple Wisdom for an Enlightened Life

Jim Larsen

Copyright © 2014 Jim Larsen
All rights reserved.
ISBN-978-0-9912920-3-5

I dedicate this book to my mother, Joan Larsen.

It is pointless to seek enlightenment. What we should do instead is seek to be enlightened. "Enlightenment' has connotations of finality, the end point of a karmic journey. How can our limited perspective know where we are on such a quest? Instead, seek to be enlightened. Enlightenment is a noun. Enlightened is an adjective. It is a state of being. It means to have found answers. Maybe you were seeking these answers , maybe you weren't. What matters is that they presented themselves to you and you paid attention, assimilating them into the totality of who you are. As such, you have discovered more about yourself, your society, and the universe.

To be enlightened is to be able to fly- to ascend above the mundane and see it from a much grander perspective as it fits into the context of the universe. Nothing is for nothing in our life. Everything has a reason and a purpose, even those things that are seemingly so small and trivial that they couldn't possible have a meaning.

Our mind gets in the way of seeing the interconnectedness of all these seemingly random and unimportant items. The mind creates obstacles to seeing these truths by way of creating assumptions that they are completely insignificant, even a hindrance to our personal discovery. In The Silence, these obstacles are overcome, for The Silence is a place of pure spirit where the ego cannot be heard. As a pure spirits, we can fly. Our mind cannot tell us we cannot.

Once we see our way past the obstacles that keep us grounded, once we are aware that we can fly and are meant to, what then? Do we actually do it? It would seem that once aware of such a thing, how could we not thrive to do so? So once we fly, once we soar as high and as mightily as we can, once we amass the strength that this provides, what do we do with this strength? Now that we are living our personal best, once we see the limits behind us, what becomes the meaning of our life? Do we achieve what we achieve in life and simply start over again in our next incarnation?

It does simply start over again with our next incarnation. However our achievements have imprinted on us a deep knowing and understanding that will serve as a foundation for the life we will live next. This is what we deposit in The Silence for ourselves that we will find again. These will be answers to future questions that will guide us on our way. Strength amassed is strength that can never be squandered. Wisdom found is wisdom that can never be forgotten. Lifetime to lifetime, what we gain will always be with us. It will always strengthen us no matter the circumstances of our earthly life, incarnation to incarnation.

The keys to an Enlightened Life are found in The Silence. When you can quiet the mind and go deep within, when you can go beyond the influence of the ego into what is true and real, you are in the realm of true wisdom and knowings. This sets the stage for an enlightened life.

If you can live by the ideas and principles you find, and not just speak of them and intellectualize about them, you are truly enlightened. If you can adapt these to your personal code of living without drawing attention to them or to seek accolades for them, you are living an enlightened life. Think about that. The need for attention and accolades are needs of the ego. If you claim to be living an "enlightened" life then are you really doing so?

To have a truly enlightened life is to live a life without the need to point to the fact that you are living by any special code or ideals. True enlightenment is transparent. True enlightenment is to be who you are as you are, simply. If you wish to live an enlightened life, just be. Just live. Don't try to be better than anybody. Don't try to be different than anybody. Just be as you are. Just listen to your own voices and your own truth. Let others sense this about you without necessarily being able to put their finger on what it is exactly. This is what it means to live an enlightened life. We all have in us the ability. We all just need to make the decision to make it so.

Knowings...

When walking amongst those who are still asleep- who have yet to waken, do you step quietly as not to disturb them? Or do you make as much noise as you can, trying in your own way to get these people to wake up? To open their eyes and see what they are missing?

Be mindful, the life we live is contingent upon the choices we make. The circumstances of our life are created by the choices that led up to it. The future is based on the choices we will make. If we are unhappy with our current life circumstances, make choices that will change it. Sometimes, be bold in the choices you make. Find the courage to make the big choices that will propel your life in an entirely different direction if you find stagnation affecting your life.

A sense of humor gives you an advantage in any situation. Remember to laugh at yourself. Laughing at yourself keeps the ego in check and gives your spirit something to smile about.

We are truly the most alive when we feel appreciated for our authentic self. Keep this in mind and be sure to express your appreciation for others. Let them feel truly alive. It makes a difference. Keep this in mind.

Always act on inspiration while it is still hot to you. Acting on it while it is hot will guarantee you will prosper with it. If you let it cool down, there is no guarantee that you can heat it up again.

The biggest regret that many people have at the end of their life is the times they gave into fear. So cut down on regrets by living fearlessly. Take those leaps of faith. Don't put up with anything that drives you crazy. Figure out what you don't understand. Don't step aside from what you feel intimidated by, but rather stand your ground in front of it and come to a mutual understanding of it so neither of you moves aside for the other out of intimidation, but rather out of respect.

A signature and sign of enlightenment is to have a genuine and sincere concern for the well-being and contentment for others even when this will not in any discernible way impact your own well-being and contentment.

Without a dream to guide you, where can you possibly go in life? Without a dream to guide you, where will you end up? Dreams are the GPS unit of our souls. They give our life direction and keep us heading to where we most need to be.

The disturbance of silence is an unacknowledged sin.

Sometimes our true nature must be evolved into. There is the destination- who we are meant to be. The journey is to get there.

Sometimes we are born far away from this destination. Our true nature may hint at what our destination may be, but we must endeavor to get there. Through a series of awakenings, we may get the idea of where we belong.

Sometimes we begin the journey feeling unsure of our steps and where we are headed. We simply have blind faith that we will be led to where we are meant to be. All we know is that where we are now is not that place. Something in our heart tugs us along. A whispered voice says "go this way." So we go. We follow an unseen force through the darkness until at last we see the light. From the journey, we evolve.

Passions can be seen as a controlled fire. It burns, but not out of control. You feed this fire with the kindling of effort and determination.

Talking badly about somebody is a pure act of ego. How could it not be? When you talk badly about somebody, you are holding yourself up as a mirror and seeing how you yourself are reflected in this person. So when you talk bad about somebody all you're really doing is saying, "Look how great I am!"

Avoid, as best you can, self-important people. You will probably never matter to them as much as you should matter to them.

You are destined for certain things. Do not settle for anything in life that does not support this or slow you down from it. Keep yourself in positions that allow you to do what is meaningful to you and allow you to put your all into your own endeavors.

We grow through pain. It happens that we have unpleasant, painful experiences, so we tense up. We draw in energy. Finally, in our minds we decide we do not like this pain, so we decide to release this tension and relax. In this relaxation, we redirect the energy that we were using to remain tense towards momentum of growth. With our minds though, we must decide to do this. We must decide to relax, and in so doing, the energy is automatically redirected.

Life is a river, meant to flow. Living is to flow with this river. What is the intensity of this river? Is it? Can you handle that? Is it too much for you? Is the river stagnant? Does it make you feel oppressed? Seek a river that has a harmonious flow for you. This is to truly appreciate life

The conformity of nonconformity generates a homogeneity of its own.

It does seem that overly talkative people have much more sensitive egos than quieter people. Overly talkative people take it personally and get upset when you suggest they are talking too much. A quiet person will just let it roll off them when people talk about how quiet they are as if this a personality defect of some kind.

Like attracts like. This is true. So, consider this in relationships. What is the condition of your heart? How is your spirit? How do you feel inside? What is the overall opinion of yourself? In order to attract to you best possible people to you, be the best version of yourself that you can be. If you feel that there are things you need to work on for yourself, then work on them. Be content with your solitude until you are complete. Whatever you can do for yourself to help yourself, do it. The more whole and complete you feel inside, the better you are able to attract somebody to you who is whole and complete too.

Sometimes you feel what goes unsaid. Your heart and your intuition fills in the blanks and gaps providing as a knowing, these unspoken words.

Once you see the big picture of life, once you are open to the divine inspirations of the universe, once you are aware of such things and they are incorporated into your daily life, it can be amazingly difficult to share space with those still trapped in the prison of their own making, the prison of their own mind. When they are obsessed with the petty and the mundane, and you yourself see beyond it, you may experience high levels of frustrations with these people, especially when they are consistent.

How do you get people beyond their obsessions? How do you get people to let go of these stuck ideas and get past their own self-imposed limitations? How do you do this without driving yourself crazy?

It is like being in a bubble with somebody. You can look up and see the world outside of the bubble and know it is doable to get outside of it, but the person you are stuck inside with cannot see it. It would be so much easier to get outside the bubble if this person would work with you, if the two of you could be a team, but as it is, this person is a hindrance.

Zoom out. Consider your daily life and the things you focus on. Consider your concerns and your preoccupations and all the things that you think matter to you. Consider these things, now zoom out just a little. Give yourself a slightly wider view of your own life. Are these things you thought were so important still so important? Now zoom out a little more. And a little more. How's the view of your life from such a wide angle? Is it giving you a much bigger perspective? Are you seeing how the small, mundane things you thought were important really are not that much so?

Every accomplishment you achieve is new strength and new power amassed. So, big or small, find something to accomplish every day.

Imagine a stone wall. This wall represents you. Now imagine cracks forming in this wall. What causes these cracks? Where do they come from? Imagine rocks and such thing being thrown at the wall causing these cracks. These rocks are demands from other people. These are often unreasonable and maybe even pointless. But they are coming at you. They are striking you, and it is having an adverse effect on you. So what can you do about this? You can live with these cracks, or you can patch them. Patch them through meditation. See them being filled with divine light and see the wall becoming pristine again. Prevent these cracks by visualizing an invisible coat of protective covering painted on the wall. Anything that hits this simply deflects off it.

In life, we shift gears. This is to go from one energy to another. The shifting can be experienced sometimes as pain as we acclimate to this new energy. In the process of shifting, there is always going to be an overlap of energies. We still feel a little of the old intermingling with the new. This can create feelings of confusion as you are not sure of where it is coming from, that which we are feeling. There can also be a sense of excitement as we know this new energy, although foreign, will propel us to higher dimensions.

Try not to make major decisions while stuck in your head. Important decisions should be made from the heart. Being stuck in your head, your thoughts will block the flow of the messages that the heart is sending. Your decision will thus be made under false pretenses. Be mindful of this. This will damage the rhythm of your life.

Our thoughts create our reality. Therefore, do not live in fear. When you live in fear, your thoughts are focused on what you are fearful of. With your thoughts focused on these things, how can you not help but to create more of it? Face your fears and move past them to be free of them.

When what is awesome and wonderful becomes ordinary and mundane, you have problems, because where do you go from there? Or maybe they are not problems after all. Maybe they just mean it is time to travel on and find something new to be fascinated by.

If you accept the anger of another, you validate it. You send the message that this anger is acceptable, even when it is not. Be careful about that.

Some people treat their life as though it is pre-lived. By staying in the past, or worrying about the future, they assume they know what the outcome will be and where they are headed. Why not surrender to the flow and let yourself simply be?

When you awaken, you are no longer in the process of awakening. This changes things. When you are in the process of awakening, you seek those things which will help you understand your true self. You are grasping onto so many different ideas and concepts, searching for those nuggets that will propel you to the understanding you most need. Once you receive all this, once you get these things, then what are you looking for? Once you have these things, then such things lose their fascination factor significantly. Therefore, what you are looking for changes, especially in terms of friendships and relationships.

When you have awakened, you are not any longer looking for people to help you understand these aspects of yourself. You are not willing to settle for people who offer less than what you are in the totality of who you are, so you tend to reject people much more easily because you simply know they will not enhance your spirit. So why settle? Why put up with it? You know the purpose of life is not to settle for such people.

You begin to seek people who witness you for who you really are, the true person you are meant to be. These people are likely to be fewer and farther between the more you embrace your awakendness. A sense of loneliness is common among the awakened and aware.

Successful people get that way by actually doing things, and not just thinking about how great life could be if everything spontaneously fell into place for them. So instead of twittling your thumbs waiting for these things to fall into place, go find these things and put them into place.

Needy people will sometimes explode energy bombs in their desperate attempt to get attention. Sometimes you may get shrapnel from this. It happens.

I ask myself, "What would Buddha do?" And the answer I hear is "Laugh, because none of it matters anyway." So I laugh.

Want to create dis-ease and disease in your life? Be rigid in your thinking. Be inflexible in your thoughts. Be so set in your ways and unbendable in your attitudes that every, even the slightest deviations ripple through you as surges of intense rippling power. True power is in the ability to bend with wind. Adapt to other ideas and other viewpoint. Evolve with each new situation. To adapt is to thrive. To adapt is to survive. Disease comes from resistance. Rigid thinking therefore causes disease. Stay flexible and stay healthy.

To be honest is to be liberated from the mind. In lies, you are focused on living and defending the lie. With honesty, there is nothing to defend. You are free. You are liberated.

You are not responsible for the random thoughts that float through your mind. What you are responsible for are what you do with them. Do you hold onto them? Do you obsess over them? Do you allow them to become worry and fear?

When it is a joyous thought, then holding onto it can lead to inspiration and happiness. There is a lot of good to be gained by holding onto a joyous thought. It's the negative ones that you must be careful of.

Be careful to not hold onto thoughts that will bring forth disharmony and discontentment. Let these thoughts float by. Perhaps there is a message to be gained from these thoughts. Process the message and move on. Don't let the thought linger, for from the simple law of attraction you will be drawing the energy of the thought to you. Do you need that much negativity coming at you? Let it go.

An enlightened person will not speak boastfully of their enlightenment. It will be a fact of who they are, not a bragging right.

It is basic mindfulness to take responsibility for your mistakes. When you make a mistake, don't automatically put your mind to assigning blame to another or try and find a way to say you didn't do it. If you make a mistake, just admit to it and move on.

People who are uncomfortable with solitude and with doing things alone have a way of being manipulative. They see their needs being met through their connections to other people, and are therefore never fully content. Because they are never fully content, they are always seeking something new, and where does this new come from? It comes from another person. What can they get from this person? They will charm this person and work their way into their consciousness to get what they can. In so doing, this other person will develop a fondness and an expectation of friendship and of love. However, it is not true. This is based only on this person's need to get what they can.

When this person's feels that they got what they needed, they move on to the next person. This leads to disharmony, discontentment, and sadness. This just means it is important to let go Release. Send these parasites on their way. Why cling to them? Do you crave the attention of a mosquito? Then why crave the attention of these people?

They establish in you what they want you to believe is friendship. The reality though is it is nothing but a siphon. Restrict the flow of this siphon for it is not fair to you. You are entitled to friendship. If what you were led to believe to be love and friendship is nothing more than petty manipulation, you have every right to put an end to it. Your heart is more valuable than that. Send compassion and forgiveness to this person and move on with your life. Of course, in the midst of this, much may be uncovered about yourself. What can you learn? How can this lead to helping you heal old wounds and move on? Explore this. Use this unique opportunity to explore these things.

Many people consider "psychic ability" as an ability to know what will happen. For some though, it is the ability to know what is beyond the veils and masks of protective covering we humans put up to shield our authentic selves. Why put up these shields? Because without them, our truth is known. An exposed truth is a vulnerable truth. It is subjected to judgment and ridicule of others. Our true self known, where can we hide? This is the bottom of who we are. This can be scary for anybody. So we cover this part of ourselves out of protection. Psychic ability is the ability to see past these protective coverings in ourselves and in others and see the hidden truth. Based on this hidden truth, what is the nature of life in the moment? How do we see this moment unfolding into the next and next and next? Psychic ability is the ability to take what we see of truth and tell a story with it as the impetus. That's all life really is, just a story.

If you have never been left behind, how will you appreciate getting caught up?

We journey to gather the fragments of our soul. Once they have been gathered, they are pieced together to reveal the picture of who we are and to get a sense of our purpose. We then fuse this together , and then we go forth as this entity our purpose creates for us.

For some, worry and fear are the dominating motivations in their life. They are so concerned that their bubble of peace will be invaded that they look for signs of attack in everything, and in so doing, they build defenses against everything. This is, of course, irrational.

Dark Night of the Soul- you enter into a dark cavernous tunnel and you must travel through it to the opening on the other side end. In this tunnel there are many demons and one incredible dragon that blocks your way. You must slay this dragon, and you must slay these demons. It is the only way to make it to the other side. You have the choice to back track, to go back the way you came, but to do so would be a weakness. To do so will do nothing to get you through this. You are only adding to your own misery, for as long as these dragons are alive, they will jab you, stick you, torment you, and torture you. To be free of them, you must slay them. There is a brightness at the other end of this tunnel. This brightness shines on the authentic you. This is where you belong. Don't fear the journey. Get there. It is for your ultimate good to do so.

Opening your heart to another is a leap of faith done without a safety net.

Pain can be a cocoon. What do you emerge from it as? How have you fortified yourself in the midst of it? How has the strength amassed within changed you?

People speak of wanting to "reach enlightenment" but how many people are truly ready for it? How many people know what it means? How many people understand that to "reach enlightenment" is a process to go through. How many people realize that it entails letting go of so many long-held beliefs and notions that are entrenched and ingrained within them? These are things that are rooted into their being and are clinging tightly. To be rid of them can cause pain. How many people are ready to face this pain? Most people, given the choice, will likely choose to remain in the dark than to prepare their selves for the light. This is their choice. Some people may begin the process, become frightened of it, and back away. Again, this is their choice. To endure the pain, to face the darkness, to see it through to the end however, has so many advantages and rewards.

So many people ask questions they already know the answer to. Why do they do this? To mask an insecurity.

If it inspires you to laugh, it is funny. If it doesn't, it's not. You decide.

Your actions can be based on reactions, or based on what you know to be true and right. Somebody may do something that you feel is inappropriate, and this is something that somehow affects you. Maybe it makes you angry, or at the very least, annoyed. You say, "I'll show them!" And do something similar that will likewise affect them. No communication happens here. Only the prolongment of a problem.

You can do this, taking it personally, or you can examine what you truly feel to be the right circumstance, how things honestly should be without taking it personally. The anger that comes to you from this other person- be the end point of it. Let it end with you. Don't perpetrate the negativity. Notice that anger is often the feeling of attack on the ego. Soften your ego so it absorbs the blow. Then let it be done. So

 much anger that people perpetrate is small and petty. To return this anger in like fashion creates the energy of anger. This anger stays stuck in itself. Only weeds grow in angry soil. This only generates enough energy to sustain the anger. This energy could be better spent going towards something positive, bright, light and good. So, be the end point of anger.

Whatever is bothering you, be willing to simply drop it. Let it go and let it be. To not will to remain stagnant, trudging through the muddy and murky landscape of nothingness. If more people would pay attention to simple mindfulness, simply being aware of how their actions are affecting those around them, there would be much less anger. Mindfulness is a root of harmony. Simple awareness, that's all it is.

A lost and damaged soul who laughs at everything to disguise the fact that she is in pain. The laughter says "look! I'm happy! I'm finding joy!" The reality is "I don't want you to know I am sad and in pain, so I am going to create this image of myself that I am happy, so you don't think I'm weak."

Intellect is attached to knowledge. . Knowledge is culturally based. It may or may not be relevant from one culture to the next. Knowledge is associated with what we consider to be facts, and with the observances of patterns that repeat in a predictable way under repeated circumstances. Knowledge gives people comfort, as the facts that create knowledge offer a seductive foundation to anchor one's trust in.

Wisdom, on the other hand, is often anchored in faith. It may or may not be anchored in any foundation of facts and knowledge. It is simply what one knows, and feels in the heart to be absolute and true. Wisdom is more personalized than knowledge. Knowledge has facts to back it up. Wisdom is backed up by personal experience.

Problems should not be limitations. Problems should be indicators of what strength needs to be amassed in order to overcome.

Every disappointment is a reminder of who you truly are. Each disappointment is an opportunity to examine the truth of your being. By examining what it is that is causing the disappointment you discover something about yourself as well as being reminded of something you already know, but perhaps forgot. How could this not be so?

Disappointment is a window to our hopes and our expectations which is an indicator of the truth of who we are, for if it bothers us to be deprived of these things, does it not point to who we see ourselves to be? If we see our lives to be incomplete without these things, then how can we not define ourselves by what hope for and what we feel deprived of?

There is really no fear except for the stories we tell ourselves. These stories are nothing but historical fiction. They are based on events of the past with the projection of how it will be repeated.

So often, we lull ourselves into a calm acceptance of our circumstances. We start out thrilled and excited, but little by little that happiness brought on by the excitement becomes eroded, not in giant blows of negativity, but by little step by step little step until we don't even realize that we are unhappy until something truly opens our eyes to the fact, and then we wonder, what's wrong here? At this point it is time to reinvent and find something new. If this is not possible due to some obligation, you must find new little things to rebuild happiness. This may not be the rebuilding of an old happiness, but rather the building of a new one within the paradigm of present conditions.

We are dual beings. We consist of mind/ego and spirit/heart. Ideally, these two will work in conjunction with one another for the greatest good of the earthly vessel. All too often though, these two are at odds with each other, one feeling wounded from the other. This is unfortunate, for with balance, a prosperity of harmony prevails.

The only time you fail is when you bother to try at all. Same goes for making mistakes. If you didn't care enough to try in the first place, you never make mistakes. So, go easy on a person who makes a mistake here and there. It just means they are trying.

It is well and good to seek empowerment, of course. This is something each and every one of us is entitled to. But to achieve it by actively seeking to dis-empower another is not the right way to go about it all.

To be truly spiritual, one must be truly grounded on the earth, for to handle and fully appreciate spiritual forces, you must have a firm grip on the earth.

Always pursue your goals without the brakes on. Put your selft in high gear and breeze through stop signs. Pursue your dreams and your passions as though you are on fire. Keep the heat of your ambitions at an all-time high. Never let your dreams cool down. Once cooled, it takes effort to them hot again. Why do this? Why put your energy towards reheating something when you can instead put your energy towards the momentum of something that is already in motion? What is in motion, keep in motion. Keep pushing it so it goes faster and faster, hotter and hotter.

To what source can any intrinsic truth be traced? There must be some infallible voice that speaks what is absolute and certain. How do we tap into this voice and hear with certainty what it is saying? You must tap into the All that is the Allness of All and listen. Will what you hear though be absolute, or will your logical mind and your ego temper it to suit your needs and desires? In this way, there is nothing absolute on the Earth. Everything on the earth is subject to interpretation. Everything on the earth is prone to misalignment. The best anybody can do is latch onto a notion of the truth that feels right to them, and maintain a loose grip on it. Allow it to be flexible, fluid, and moveable. Do not be too stringent in any belief. Allow for alterations based on new attitudes, new beliefs, and new interpretations.

Say this: "You will have to forgive my imperfections. I am not here to impress you or to be perfect in your eyes, or to be perfect at all. I am not here to be perfect, but rather to perfect some piece or other of my spirit the best I can. This has nothing to do with impressing you, but everything to do with living the best way I can regardless of your opinions of me. That's just how it is and the way it goes."

Karma is not an intellectual pursuit. You cannot simply assign "karma" to this and "karma" to that. Karma is something so deep and so spiritual and something beyond our mind's ability to truly grasp the intricacies of how can we possibly know how karma is playing out in our life? Much of what we attribute to karma and "instant karma" is simply our reaction to a feeling of guilt within ourselves or a feeling of self-riotousness towards others. As long as we do what we feel is right in any given situation and in life itself, we don't need to worry about karma. Just let karma work itself out.

Develop a mindfulness of silence, asking "Do the words I am about to say need to be said? Are they worthy of the silence they will fill?" If the answer is an honest no, allow them to go unsaid. Nobody will even miss them. If though, the answer is yes, speak them. Allow others to consider them and find an appropriate response, if one is needed. This is to have a mindfulness of silence. Respect those who practice it and allow yourself to emulate them. This is proper communication. This is to be heard in a meaningful way- heard because your words have volume, and are not just loud. Heard because there is a meaningfulness in your words, not just a grab for attention. For some, it will take practice. For others it will be second nature. For some, it will be a lesson that is learned the hard way. However it comes for you, make it a lifestyle.

Those that like to act better than you, let them be better than you. Just step aside and let them go by. Go your own way and shine your own brilliance in your own way. And you don't even have to do it to prove anything to anybody.

Don't look for happiness through deities. When you do this, you only look for happiness through the idea of deities. Look for happiness within. When you do this, you awaken the deities within. Now you experience the deities that are meaningful to you, whether or not you can even name them.

The reality that is for you may be to another, the reality that could be as they look to you with admiration.

A butterfly that never leaves the cocoon will never spread its wings and fly. Nobody will ever say, "Ah. Look at that butterfly." Once you are transformed, fly away. Take your brilliance and share it with the world.

Eventually your shortcomings catch up to you and you have to answer them. You will stand in judgment of them. They will demand to know why you chose fear instead of action. They will want to know why you let petty and mundane things dictate the actions of your life, and more importantly they will want to know with what convictions you will move forward with your life to put these shortcomings behind you. What will your answers be?

When you stand and face your greatest fear without backing down, when you let all the emotions that this brings up wash over you without drowning you, when you feel that indeed, they are drowning you, but you find the strength and fortitude to fight your way to the surface and not suffocate from it, you are truly ready to evolve into the person you were always meant to be.

Anywhere you are on earth is Heaven when you live the best version of yourself.

Be careful not to fall into complacency. If you do though, find yourself in the pit of complacency, endeavor not to stay there. Climb out. Complacency is the death of the imagination. Don't let yourself die so easily.

How can one heal if they never get out of the environment that caused them to need the healing to begin with? How can one heal if they stay around the people that are causing them distress and pain? Sometimes getting away from a painful environment is the best way to see the pain it is causing you. By being in a new environment and noticing that something is missing and asking yourself what that is, "What's missing?" and discovering that it is the pain that is missing is ta good way to instigate healing within yourself.

A dream wouldn't find you if it didn't think you could do it justice.

We follow gurus. We listen to everything they say. We treat their words as though they are infallible. At some point though, the truly wise come to the realization that they have abundant wisdom all their own. They are completely capable of being their own guru, perhaps even a guru for others.

No guru, though, should seek followers. Anybody seeking followers should be avoided. Offer what you have to offer. Get it out there in any way you can. Then let people find you. Those in need of what you have to offer will, via serendipity, find you. Any attempt to force it on anybody will make you seem as a shyster to any legitimate guru and limit your audience to limited thinkers. This does no good. This only validates some empty and worthless part of yourself.

Intuition is a learning process. When following your intuition you follow and are guided by impulses. These impulses of course are guided by the spirit and the heart, and thus must be interpreted by the mind. To be truly intuitive, we will experience impulses that are new to us. We will feel things that are foreign and unusual. To someone who is unaware, these feelings will be thought of as something to be dismissed and not given thought to. To somebody who is aware, however, they are to be paid attention to and followed. Where are these impulses taken me? What messages do they have? What do they want me to know? What can I learn from them? The trick is to identify them and learn when there is something to pay attention to them.

Some people rely on going through life playing a character. It is better to be authentic and present your real true self to the world. If you do not present your real true self to the world, people will not respond to you in an authentic way.

Dreams come true through persistence. Dreams do not come true from thoughts alone. They require concentrated devotion. Hold the vision of the dream and take actual steps to make them come true. Progress towards a dream's fulfillment equates to empowerment.

Follow no gospel except for the one you find within. This is comprised of your own knowings and wisdom, accumulated through many lifetimes of gathering, collecting, analyzing and understanding.

Good coworkers are people you work with, not people you work around.

We absorb and experience energy from others. It may or may not be "good energy" or "bad energy" but energy that is simply foreign to us, and often times anything that is foreign to us will be uncomfortable.

Each step we take brings us one step closer to our death. So why be in a hurry?

Where does the spirit go while the body is asleep? A sleeping body is the spirit's chance to roam unhindered and unobligated to a logical mind.

We all have a perspective of the world, and this perspective is contingent upon our experiences, expectations, desires, hopes, fears, and preoccupations. It is though art, writing, music, and all other such talents that we share our perspective with others. In sharing our perspectives, we give others the opportunity to experience the benefit of them, whether they agree or not. In not agreeing, the opportunity is created to truly define one's own perspective by analyzing and giving thought to what it is they do not agree with. By agreeing, one's own perspective is strengthened by validation. This generates a synergy of power as a multitude of people feel validated by their viewpoint without having to struggle to be understood.

This though, does create the risk of complacency and homogeneity as so many people sharing the same viewpoint stop looking for differentiations and when a differentiation does come, it is viewed as a threat to a way that has long been established. Now, change to this viewpoint is difficult to achieve without a tremendous amount of people sharing an opposing viewpoint who are willing to speak up and express their opposition. In time, this opposing viewpoint will gain a foothold in the minds and psyches of the given population and become integrated into the given society just as the original viewpoint it originally opposed which by now has been altered and changed in reaction to this opposition.

Most of us do not live in pain. We live in the memory of pain which triggers a fear of pain. If we examine our real true feeling, we will see that all is well. It's the anticipation that pain will come based on certain emotional triggers that causes distress. Follow the shadow back to the light and experience that original pain fully to be done with it because that anticipation can have an unfortunate effect on you. It can keep you trapped in a fog. You are not seeing the true reality of a situation, that the people in your life in the here and now mean you no harm. They have no idea of the pain you were once in and that they are reminding you of it. Yet, you are reacting to them as if you expect the worse from them. This will put an edge on your energy that they will feel and react to. It will seem like there is a problem with you. They will wonder why you are as you are.

Sometimes we deny our intuition simply because the intuition we are feeling is something we would rather not face. We tell ourselves "No. That can't be." But that changes nothing. What is coming at us is coming at us no matter what. We cannot change it. It is destined and ordained. If our intuition feels negative to us, we should use this as a chance to prepare ourselves mentally for the challenges ahead.

Sometimes a desire can be to be right as opposed to another person. Sometimes it can be to establish physical or mental or even spiritual dominance over another. Get past this need. To be perfect within yourself for the sake of yourself without the need of comparison to other is to be enlightened.

I am, therefore I am.

Apologies mean less and less the more they pile up.

A chick that stays in the egg will suffocate and die. Know when it is time to leave. Know when you have amassed the strength and transformations that you need for the next chapter of your life.

For there to be evolution, there must be revolution. This is a personal thing, a personal revolution. This is to take stock of your own limiting beliefs, agents of procrastination, and ideas that are telling us why something cannot or should not be done, or why everything is just fine the way it is without any need to change, and then just be complacent, even though in your heart and your spirit is fully aware that things are missing, that something about this paradigm is unsatisfactory and just not right. You know this. You feel this. You sense that there can be more, that life can be exciting.

When we not only wake up to our purpose, not just partially fully, but completely fully. and to live fully is to be on fire, to have your sparks become a fire, a flame, an inferno. For this to happen, we each must eliminate all that is convincing us that we cannot. You must have the attitude of a warrior. You must instigate an internal revolution. You must face these agents of negativity head on and eliminate them. They have been in control for too long. They have been telling you false facts long enough.

These false facts are that what you are trying to accomplish are not doable, and that your station in life is set. You will always be this, that, or whatever you are. Or it may tell you can always do it tomorrow. That it will take care of itself… tomorrow, tomorrow, it will happen. Don't think about it today, let tomorrow handle it.

Tomorrow comes, tomorrow comes, tomorrow comes, and nothing happened. Realize this- tomorrow doesn't care. You are putting your destiny and your purpose in the hands of an empty entity when you place it in the hands of tomorrow.

You know what you want. You do. Your heart has been telling you for ages, maybe even screaming at you. But there's your mind convincing you that you can't have it, or that it will "just happen." The mind is not one with the spirit. You must get past this.

This is the spirit's revolution, to get past the mind's reasoning as to why something can't be done, or that it can be done later, and then fly. The spirit is meant to fly, so don't let the mind cage it. The spirit must revolt and break free of the cage that the mind will put it in. This is the revolution that will lead to evolution, for when we are following our spirit's desire, we accomplish our missions. By accomplishing our missions, we evolve. That's how simple it is.

So many people ask questions they already know the answer to. Why do they do this? To mask an insecurity.

I would rather be at the end of a long line sometimes than to endure the same old same old at the front of it.

To an empath, the concept of personal space takes on many other dimensions.

Get out of thoughts of survival and into the creative flow, and soon your creativity will provide an abundance of fortune and prosperity. You'll see.

Essentially, it boils down to keeping your focus and your attention away from ideas of why something cannot happen. Now, all there are is reasons why it can, which in a sense is the same vibration that it has as if it already happened. Now there is no reason for it not to.

Anger has a way of being self-perpetuating, gaining momentum and picking up speed when left unchecked.

The day you make the conscious decision to live based on your own strength and your own power and not give into fear and intimidation, and to not feel a need to force your ideas and attitudes onto others, nor to give into those being forced onto you, is the day you truly awaken. This is, in earnest, the first day of the rest of your life.

Wisdom is found out of doors, amongst the wind, the plants and the trees. To become wise, do not stay indoors behind a desk and a computer screen. No, get out doors if you want to experience true wisdom.

A dream is just a dream. It's your interpretation of it that makes it a nightmare.

Still waters run deep. Be an infinite well.

Pain forces awareness. Areas that you generally pay no attention to or simply take for granted suddenly are in the forefront of your awareness when it is in pain. Pain forces mindfulness. It forces you to notice and analyze these things you would not ordinarily pay attention to. This is one true power of pain, to get you to appreciate all the parts of the whole, all the pieces and all the aspects that add up to who you are, and to empathetically appreciate how you fit in with others and the totality of who they are.

Surrender your ego and accept that there is more to who you are than mere mind and you will grow as a spirit and a person and as an influence throughout the universe exponentially as you allow your team of divine helpers and guides to work with you and to work through you. This will strengthen you in human form, as a spirit, the species in general, and ripple through the cosmos to points you can only imagine.

Choose the day you want to have, and then have it. Want a good day? Make the decision to have a good day, then make sure everything you do supports you having a good day. Want a bad day? Make the decision to have a bad day, then make sure everything you do supports you having a bad day. It's your choice. Have any kind of day you want.

Sometimes you have to burn some bridges if you ever hope to get where you are going. Otherwise, you'll only end up slipping backwards. Keep your momentum moving forward.

The mark of a true leader is not his or her power over people, but rather their power to harmonize and synergize.

As long as you react to the negativity of others, you remain stagnant in their negativity. Rise above negativity and react from above it all. Gain perspective before reacting, otherwise you are just feeding the negativity and making its source stronger. Do not give it more power. Do all it takes to be its endpoint. To do so is true strength.

Use your inner self to shape your outer self. In this way, you will become who you are truly meant to be.

A quiet nature is not necessarily an indication of shyness. A quiet nature can just as easily be an indication of a sense of discernment of what is necessary to be said. It can be an indicator of awareness, a realization of how your words and your presence affect others.

So many people want to bend the world to fit their needs. They got it backwards. They need to adjust their selves to the world at hand. Accept what cannot be changed.

As long as you're happy, you'll be fine.

Sometimes living in a situation of "better safe than sorry" really equates to "let's create fear and live in that fear." Sometimes just leave well enough alone. Don't create a problem just because you have a clever idea for a solution that you want to make fit somewhere.

Never trust anybody who uses the word "Amazing" more than three times in a minute when describing a canoe.

There are a number of realities. The one we experience is the one that "is." But what of the others? These are the ones that "could be."

We may ponder the could be realities and wish to experience them. To experience them is entirely possible- writers, artists and musicians (to name a few) do it all the time. When dissatisfied with the reality that is, and this dissatisfaction causes suffering, it is worthwhile to explore the reality that could be.

Do this without limiting yourself. Explore all the boundaries of the reality that could be. Find the elements that you truly believe would enhance the reality that is, and bring ithem back with you. Find a way. Incorporate them into a project or just keep them in your soul as determination. This determination is a seed you found in the reality of could be, propagated in the reality that is.

A shadow can be a question you are simply afraid to seek an answer to. Perhaps this is an issue you have experienced before and it was painful to you. You are now faced with a similar situation where you fear it may go in the direction of pain again, but at the same time, it could easily go in the direction of positivity and happiness. So as you are looking at this situation, you are conditioned to expect the negative outcome. This is fear. This is worry.

But this is not a dark shadow void of light. This is a shadow in its last seconds of darkness before the light overtakes it. Instead of fearfully retreating from it, barrel through it. Be surprised by it. By retreating you deny yourself the opportunity to prosper from the positive outcome. By facing this fear you get through the shadow. So, when faced with the fear that a situation will go in a negative direction, visualize the light. Instead of letting the fear slow you down, let the optimism of the light propel you.

Use the light as fuel to drive you. In this way you will succeed. In this way, you will excel. By accepting fear, you will always stay stuck, stay stagnate. In life, we are meant to move forward. Always move towards the light. Never stay stuck in the darkness of the shadow. Don't let fear rule you. Don't let fear dictate your growth.

Some people will use confusion as an opportunity to develop faith. They will trust that the answers required will fall into place. Others will treat confusion as an attack, and desperately scramble to fight off these elements sent to disrupt their perfect peace of mind.

What happens when you are constantly hot and cold hot and cold hot and cold with somebody? Eventually, you just become tepid to them. It happens.

Everything you do is a step in the right direction. The question becomes, how quickly do you take these steps?

To an empath a drug-infused person, especially in a work environment, can be a nightmare. An empath, whether consciously aware or not, feels the energy from the people in their close proximity. This can be a good feeling when these people are complete and have a good sense about them.

Drugs though, damage this. The aura of these people are damaged and jagged. There a number of gaps and holes in this aura. The empath feels these jags and senses these holes.

Drugs enhance a person's dullness. They dull down a person's spark and diminish it significantly. An empath feels a person's spark. To sense their diminished spark can be quite depressing and unsettling. A true empath will know and sense the strength of another's powers and abilities. It can be confusing and frustrating to witness the diminishing of their spark and the intentional deadening of potential. A true empath will know the full potential of the people whose energy they are absorbing.

Trust is one of those things that every so often needs to be rethought, realigned, reinterpreted and overhauled.

Don't blame the mirror if you don't like the reflection.

Remember as you go with the flow, that the flow has many branches. The flow is as a river with its current ebbing ever forward. This river has many outlets. As an outlet approaches that is desirable to you, you can maneuver towards it with the force of your intentions and will.

Each of these represents an opportunity, a choice. There are many flows to choose from in the Universe, and be it known to you that each will eventually reach the ocean, an ocean. So go with the flow, it will in time take you where you need to be. It all empties into and contributes to the universal oneness.

Going with the flow can lead you to this ocean. Resisting the flow slows you from it. When there is much resistance, when entire societies resist, much turbulence ensues. There are many rivers, many flows. If the flow you find yourself in is incongruent with your desires and happiness, make a choice. Make a decision. Edge yourself over to one of the branches, or perhaps move yourself to another river all together. Be in a river, a flow with like-minded people to achieve maximum happiness and enjoyment in life.

One of the first things you need to do on the path to enlightenment is to get the voices of those around you out of your head. These are the voices that are telling you what you must do. These voices will tell you that something is wrong when it's perfectly right. These are the voices that will not speak the truth to you. They will not speak your truth. Your truth is unique to you, for the mission you were born to fulfill is yours and only yours. Your inner voice and the voices of your divine helpers speak to you in such a way that keeps you on the path to fulfill your mission. They speak by impulses, flashed of inspiration, and any number of ways that may not be perceived by anybody else but you. Listen to these voices, be mindful of them, honor them. It is for your own greatest good that you do. Those that do not know or understand you- let your inner voices drown them out.

Enlightenment is about remembering. When we remember who we truly are, what we came to the earth for, what we truly know, we are truly enlightened. Little reminders are placed here and there, and we gather them. They are each a piece to the puzzle. When we collect these pieces, we remember. This is to be enlightened.

Good leadership is for the good of the people, not for the glorification of the ego of the leader.

You can't force inspiration, nor can you impose it on somebody. Inspiration happens without coaxing. It can be nurtured by the attention you give it, but you cannot force it happen.

When achieving a goal, do not approach it with an attitude of "I probably can't do this, but I'll do my best, because who knows?" Approach it with an attitude that in a perfect world, this has already been done, and now I am simply catching up to it.

Living without walls means living without boundaries. Without boundaries, what are the obstacles? Living without boundaries means being able to rise to the level of your own greatness. How many people though, do that? How many people, when presented with the opportunity to get past restrictions and blocks, truly open their wings and fly? How many, in reality, fold their wings and settle into the lowest common denominator of their own life and never really become what they are truly capable of becoming?

How many simply rely on old patterns, old needs of restrictions to keep their selves in what their mind tells them is their personal best, when in reality this is just a grounding, an anchor. This is the mind. The mind is an anchor. While the spirit is capable and meant to fly, the mind keeps it close to the ground. The mind will ground the spirit.

Why? Why is it allowed to do this? Because the mind has a way of seizing control. We are conditioned to believe that the mind is the most important component of the human construct. This is folly. This is unfortunate. This is what must be unlearned if enlightenment is to be achieved.

True enlightenment is all about getting past the idea that we are limited. This means that we are, intrinsically speaking, born enlightened. If it is our mind that keeps us grounded, keeps us seeing our enlightened state, then obviously one purpose of our life is to find our way or ways past that.

Focus your gaze on a static object in front of you and become aware of the activity in your peripheral vision, and you realize what an ant colony this life really is.

Inner peace and contentment come from doing what you know is right, following your own internal guidance even when those around you make it difficult to do so.

If you are unhappy with what you are doing, isn't it an obligation to yourself to find something that you are happy with? You are, after all, the steward of your own soul. Whose responsibility but your own is your happiness?

Others will attach to you their needs of you. Often, you may find it completely congruent with your own. You can be with the team or in a partnership just fine. Other times it may seem overwhelming, like vampires have fixed themselves on you and are sucking the life force out of you.

When this is the case, joy is lost. Bleakness and dimness set in. This is the case because you allow it to be the case. Life, however, is meant to be lived in the light. Happiness is an absolute birth right. Darkness serves its purpose, of course. In the darkness we sleep. In the darkness we go within and learn of ourselves.

In the darkness imposed by others, we too learn of ourselves. We see what opposes us. We discover our true nature such that we discover the reflections that disturb us. What is it to be bothered by another, but to discover a part of our self that we are discontent with? Discover these discontentments and address them. Learn what you can in the darkness and move to the light.

In life, it is good to have at least one thing you do just for you. This is something that you don't have to explain to anybody, even the people you are closest to. When the rest of the world gets you down, when life seems just simply difficult, you have this to go to just for you. You can uplift yourself and feel better knowing nobody is going to criticize or undermine you in this.

A feeling of discomfort is just another limitation falling away.

One of the worst lessons you can teach somebody is that they should just keep their mouth shut. Let people say what they want. This makes them feel valued. Don't send the message that nothing they say is important or of value. This feeling will sink in and stay with them for many many days to follow. Don't undermine people in this way. Let them express their selves. Somewhere within their core is brilliance. Let them find it. Let them express it. Help them by not immediately dismissing everything they want to say.

The true strength of any guru is their ability to coax wisdom out of others, more so than any need to impose their wisdom and/or ideas on others.

Peace of mind, contentment, and true happiness should not be treated as luxuries. These are birthrights. Each and every person is entitled.

Dreams require focus. Try not to divert or split your energies too much when working towards one. Too much diversion will only dilute the energy used to fulfill your dreams. Stay focused and you will achieve success.

Sometimes we may feel unempowered. Sometimes we feel small and unimportant within the context of the whole. In this case, examine the "whole" you feel unimportant in. Ask yourself, "Why am I here?" There are so many other "wholes" you can involve yourself in. Why settle for one that makes you feel like less than you deserve to be?

Tap into your dreams. Find them. Use them as the roots for the power you will grow into. Let your dreams sink deep into the earth and become solid. From them let your reality grow with strength and surety.

Never, under any circumstances settle for disempowerment. When you are sure of your dreams, there is no reason to settle for less. When you are sure of your dreams you are strong. You have strength. You can propel yourself to and beyond new horizons and new plateaus. When you follow your dreams, you are not just along for the ride on the planet. No, you are steering the planet in the direction of your own destiny.

If you are not proactive, you will only end up spinning your wheels. The more you spin, the deeper the rut becomes. Make the choice immediately to actively remove yourself from any troubling circumstances immediately and be free if it right away.

Wherever you are, remember it is but one minuscule spec on the map. If you are discontent, there are uncountable other minuscule specs you can explore.

When you undermine somebody you rob them of the chance to be the best version of their self. Don't do that.

All the energy put into making yourself seem right often results in you looking stupid instead.

Our perfection is limited by what triggers us. A step towards enlightenment is to identify these triggers and move beyond them.

Every deity represents a path to a higher truth. They are not the truth of and in their self. They are simply a gateway to a higher truth. By appreciating and examining what these deities represent, you can expand your own ideas and awareness of your own truth. By expanding your own truth, you create God in the form that is relevant to you as you seek a God that fits the mold your truth has created. To create a truth that is molded by another's idea of God will be a mistake. Seek wisdom, not dogma. Through wisdom, a truth will emerge. Through dogma, frustration will develop.

Shadows contrast the light. Shadows give a foundation to and support the light. Without shadows, would there even be light?

Try not to think of success as an accumulation of anything external, not materialistic belongings or money in the bank, or titles, certificates, or accolades. Try to think of success as what you have gained within. Think of it as what strength you have gained and what wisdom you have amassed. Let success be determined by the strengthening of your spirit.

When you obsess, you are denying the flow. You are resisting a truth. The truth is that this which you are obsessing over exists in the false reality that you have created. You created a reality in which this object has a heightened sense of importance. So you cling tightly to this. You don't allow for the flow. Release your grip. Surrender to the river and to the flow. If this thing you have been gripping is important, if it is intrinsic to your wellbeing, it will follow you in the flow. Trust. Let go and flow. Successful people know when to let go of an idea or a concept that they are clinging to, and edge their self to the next one, or another one. Truly successful people know when to let go.

People love to validate their inadequacies. They do this by making excuses. Rather than simply admit to their laziness or their shortcomings as they originate from within, they attach an outside force to it.

Why do they do this? This is attached to the ego. They are incapable of, or perhaps unwilling to admit what they fear will be an inadequacy. This is often in the face of the reality that most intelligent and thinking people witnessing them can clearly see their inadequacy and are more than willing to overlook it and forgive them. Now, the excuse making is added to the tally of what is perceived as inadequate.

Often, we are surrounded by these people . This is our world. This is the paradigm. We no longer live in a world of authenticity and truth. What we are living with is a world full of people projecting the image they want to be perceived as- as perfect beyond measure with forces outside of their selves conspiring to make them look bad and create blocks between them and perfection. What these people fail to realize is, if they would just face and admit the truth from the beginning, they would garner the respect and the admiration of those around them on a much more significant level. But instead, they project falseness. This becomes endemic as nobody wants to appear weaker than anybody else, all of whom are projecting a falseness.

A sensitive person will pick up on this. A sensitive person will likely feel sick around these people as they absorb the desperation to be noticed as perfect, however false the projection is. People need to realize they are as perfect as they need to be without making these excuses.

Sometimes things are best understood in reflection, when we look back at them. When we are in the midst of a situation, we may not know all the facts. It is when we are beyond it and have a grander perspective. When we see how a multitude of influences have played their part in the situation does it make sense. This is a reflective energy.

Likewise, when we see our reflection from another person, we may be surprised at what we see, what we learn about our self. In our minds, we imagine ourselves to be a certain way and we convince ourselves that this is the truth of who we are. But do other people have this same vision of us? Who are we to them may be completely different from who we are to ourselves. We see ourselves reflected in their attitude towards us, actions towards us, and reactions to us.

The trick to living, really, is not to try to be this or that, but to go with the natural flow of who you really are and flourish within it.

It is a basic human desire, need, to be seen and witnessed for our passion and love. For those stuck in survival mode though, this desire, need becomes endemic. You will see that they need constant witnessing and validation for nearly everything they do, every move they make. This is a mark of one who has not yet awakened. This is somebody who has a ways to go to be awakened and fully actualized. They will feel sad and insecure when left alone or by there self, for there is no one to see them, no one to validate them, no one to witness them and give them a score on how they are doing. They need a gauge, somebody to impress.

For one who has awakened, or is in the process of awakening, however they can be their own internal gauge. They can give a self-assessment of their ideas and actions. These people will strive for accomplishments, and present these accomplishments to the world boldly and confidently. They are not concerned with the petty and mundane thoughts that others have of them or for their actions, so they do not seek validation. These people are comfortable in their own skin with their own ideas and thoughts.

They will give space to others to do their thing, pursue their goals, and will recognize and appreciate true greatness in others, but will have standards for such things. A truly awakened person will not encourage mediocrity in others. A truly awakened person will bring forth the star quality of others and encourage this to shine brightly.

Life lesson to be learned- don't let people get to you. As soon as you learn this, you can move on from it and be free of the circumstances that synchronisticaly line up to give you the opportunity to learn from it.

Be the antithesis of what you deplore and look upon with disdain. Know that there are others also looking upon these things with disdain and disgust. Let them see you as the alternative to it. In this way, you will shine by comparison. This means to remain above without sinking to the level of these disdainful people.

To live an enlightened life is to assess and appreciate the strengths of others without the sense that they magnify your own weaknesses.

Whatever an energetic feeling feels like to you, that's what it is. If it feels like a thousand and one bugs are infesting your brain, then a thousand and one bugs are infesting your brain. Now you have a way of dealing with it. How would you deal with a thousand and one bugs infesting your brain?

To view and understand yourself, not as opposed to others, but as powerful within yourself is true strength.

No questions. Answers only lead to judgment. Let's not have any of that.

It is a rude thing to do, to expect somebody to be a mind reader and hold it against them when they are not.

An economy of favors. Don't shirk from putting your energy or your time into something for another person even when you expect nothing in return. Even though you expect nothing in return, somehow someway, your energy will be given back to you. Somehow, some way, whether consciously aware of the act or not, your favor will be returned.

Trees give voice to the wind. To benefit fully from the wisdom of the wind, dwell amongst the trees.

Grant others an Amnesty of Forgiveness. Wipe the slate of grudges clean and fill it only with love.

Integrity means to do what you know is the right thing even when it is more convenient to do the wrong thing, no matter if anybody is watching or not.

Being enlightened is not about what you know, but more about what you do with what you know. Do you live by the principles of your knowings, or are they simply passive ideas for you?

www.ingramcontent.com/pod-product-compliance
Lightning Source LLC
Chambersburg PA
CBHW071504040426
42444CB00008B/1489